Josh Nathan was raised until adulthood in Baptist and Methodist teachings. He later adopted Pentecostal doctrines which in reality did not essentially conflict with his protestant background. He is currently head of his church's Sunday school department and the youth church. He writes monthly short sermons which are published in the church bulletin. Josh is blessed with a lovely wife and two wonderful boys.

FAILED PRAYERS

Josh Nathan

FAILED PRAYERS

AUSTIN MACAULEY

A CIP catalogue record for this title is
available from the British Library.

ISBN 978 1 905609 20 8

www.austinmacauley.com

First Published (2008)
Austin & Macauley Publishers Ltd.
25 Canada Square
Canary Wharf
London
E14 5LB

Printed & Bound in Great Britain

DEDICATION

To the Ancient of days and most merciful one.

To my lovely and longsuffering wife

To my boys who both are the excellency of power and glory

ACKNOWLEDGEMENTS

My sincerest and heartfelt appreciation goes to the Almighty one who supplied grace, vision, revelation and stamina to complete this work.

I thank my wife and lifelong companion who has been the singular most influential motivator and without whom I would not have found the courage to finish this task.

I appreciate the endurance of my boys whose time I stole on countless occasions in order to stay focussed.

Finally I would like to thank Annette Longman and her colleagues at Austin & Macauley for publishing my work.

Shalom

Josh Nathan

TABLE OF CONTENTS

Introduction

We all must have at one time or the other, prayed fervently and in sound faith for something important to us in our Christian experience to which we did not receive an answer from God. We applied the word of God, we were not living in sin at the time, we fasted and were expectant, and we even asked others to join faith with us to receive this thing from God to no avail. At such times, we must have felt very dejected and disillusioned about God and probably our standing in God. It doesn't help either when people tell us that we did not receive our desired result because it was probably not God's will, or that we should have had more faith or that it was due to our sins, and all other such explanations.

The truth of the matter is that an unanswered prayer remains an unanswered prayer which is not very encouraging for a believer. We all desire to get good results whenever we pray to God so it is only right to be sad when we do not get results having prayed in faith.

I recognise that there are certain prayers which may not be answered yet because God is asking us to wait for them, and that there are some which God rejects because they are not in line with His plans for our lives. The point of the matter is: whatever class or category our prayer falls into when they are unanswered, they appear as disappointments at first until there is clarity about their status. If God does not give you a good thing that you sincerely need, God has enough integrity to offer you sound counsel as to why He has not given it to you yet, or what the consequences of giving it to you at that moment may be.

I am not talking about such prayers rather I am talking about prayer points to which you simply never got any response, explanation or result. The big question I would like to ask here is: "What happens to our unanswered requests?

I am sure that there must be millions of requests we have made in our lives which, though predicated on faith, remain unanswered till now. What do we or what can we indeed do about such requests? Do we simply do the easiest thing and forget about them? Should we retroactively ask God for explanations or should we be angry and discouraged that we prayed to God and did not receive answers?

I reiterate that I am not discussing unanswered prayers occasioned by sin, lack of faith or prayers that remain unanswered because God has a higher purpose. These categories will be discussed in the latter part of this book; I am talking about prayer for simple things in life which are rational, essential and time-governed. For instance, as a young teenager, you may have asked God to give you a bicycle like other teens you knew, but you never got the bicycle.

You may have asked God to give you a breakthrough for a particular thing which you needed for a specific time or event, but that time or event is now past and you never got the answer. Obviously a bicycle is of no use to you now as an adult even if God decided to give you one, also should you get the breakthrough now it is probably useless as it is out of time and redundant. It is such prayer points that I am talking about. You may have been very sick and asked God to heal you to no avail until one of your limbs is now amputated. The question on your mind would no doubt be "what possible glory can God get from me having my limb?" The answer to that question is simple, "God takes no glory for you being amputated, because He is Jehovah Rapha, the Lord your healer (Exodus 5:26)." People say that "every disappointment is a blessing" nothing could be farther from the truth. I put it simply, every disappointment is a disappointment.

God finds no glory in our unanswered prayers. He takes no pleasure in our disappointments. He wants us to live in good health and prosperity. 3 John 1:2 puts it very succinctly.

Beloved, I wish above all things that thou mayest prosper and be in health, even as thy soul prospereth.

So I repeat my question, "what happens to unanswered prayers?" Or should I ask "what should we do when our prayers of faith are unanswered?" The answers to these questions will be found in the word of God. In the next few pages I will attempt to discuss certain biblical accounts to examine how people like us dealt with prayer requests

Chapter 1

Case Studies on Persistence

<u>Abraham - Genesis 18:23-32</u>

23 And Abraham drew near, and said, Wilt thou also destroy the righteous with the wicked? 24 Peradventure there be fifty righteous within the city: wilt thou also destroy and not spare the place for the fifty righteous that are therein? 25 That be far from thee to do after this manner, to slay the righteous with the wicked: and that the righteous should be as the wicked, that be far from thee: Shall not the Judge of all the earth do right? 26 And the LORD said, If I find in Sodom fifty righteous within the city, then I will spare all the place for their sakes. 27 And Abraham answered and said, Behold now, I have taken upon me to speak unto the Lord, which am but dust and ashes: 28 Peradventure there shall lack five of the fifty righteous: wilt thou destroy all the city for lack of five? And he said, If I find there forty and five, I will not destroy it. 29 And he spake unto him yet again, and said, Peradventure there shall be forty found there. And he said, I will not do it for forty's sake. 30 And he said unto him, Oh let not the Lord be angry, and I will speak: Peradventure there shall thirty be found there. And he said, I will not do it, if I find thirty there. 31 And he said, Behold now, I have taken upon me to speak unto the Lord: Peradventure there shall be twenty found there. And he said, I will not destroy it for twenty's sake. 32 And he said, Oh let not the Lord be angry, and I will speak yet but this once: Peradventure ten shall be found there. And he said, I will not destroy it for ten's sake.

Abraham is commonly referred to as 'the father of faith'; personally, I believe that there is no truer statement than that. Abraham had a prayer request which he put before God and refused to give up until his purpose was achieved. The big question here is "why did Abraham ask God to spare the people of Sodom and Gomorrah?" Could it be because he loved the two cities or was it because his nephew, Lot, and his family resided there? Whatever Abraham's reason, it is evident that he persevered until he was satisfied. God still destroyed Sodom and Gomorrah despite Abraham's intercession, but He spared Lot's family. My personal view on the subject is that Abraham was desperate to save his nephew's family and God saw his heart and decided to honour his request as a result of his fervency.

<u>Jacob - Genesis 32:26-28</u>

26 And he said, Let me go, for the day breaketh. And he said, I will not let thee go, except thou bless me. 27 And he said unto him, What is thy name? And he said, Jacob. 28 And he said, Thy name shall be called no more Jacob, but Israel: for as a prince hast thou power with God and with men, and hast prevailed.

The account above is yet another demonstration of an ardent attitude in prayer. Jacob had just endured a prolonged encounter with a divine being without giving up. As a matter of fact, the divinity commended Jacob for his power with men and even with God. Jacob refused to let the man go because he knew that he was divinity, and was therefore capable of blessing him. Jacob was not going to let go of such a great opportunity, he held on to his request until he received the blessing he sought so desperately.

We must learn a lesson from this account because, each time we enter into God's presence to obtain mercies at the time of need, we are more or less in the same position as Jacob. We are in the presence of divinity and should be aware of the capability of God to bless us, we should not allow ourselves to be put off if it seems at first that God is reluctant to bless us. We should remind him of His promises and pester Him, complain to Him, disturb Him, as it were, until He grants our request. The more desperate you, are the more you are likely to hold on to God until He grants your request.

Moses - Exodus 33:12-17

12 And Moses said unto the LORD, See, thou sayest unto me, Bring up this people: and thou hast not let me know whom thou wilt send with me. Yet thou hast said, I know thee by name, and thou hast also found grace in my sight. 13 Now therefore, I pray thee, if I have found grace in thy sight, shew me now thy way, that I may know thee, that I may find grace in thy sight: and consider that this nation is thy people. 14 And he said, My presence shall go with thee, and I will give thee rest. 15 And he said unto him; If thy presence go not with me, carry us not up hence. 16 For wherein shall it be known here that I and thy people have found grace in thy sight? Is it not in that thou goest with us? So shall we be separated, I and thy people, from all the people that are upon the face of the earth. 17 And the LORD said unto Moses, I will do this thing also that thou hast spoken: for thou hast found grace in my sight, and I know thee by name.

In the account above, we learn of how Moses intervened when God was determined to destroy the Israelites in the wilderness. The Israelites deserved God's punishment for their many atrocities against God. God was simply fed up with them and was going to vent His anger on them. Moses was in a position to simply have accepted the situation as it stood. Instead he prayed to God to spare his people and reminded him about what God had said about him (Moses). He then used this testimony about himself from God has a platform to intercede for the Israelites. God then said in verse 14 that He would spare Moses and that His presence will go with him. Moses was not, however, satisfied that God was going to spare just him alone and not the Israelites, and in verse 15 Moses said to God "I would like your presence to go with all of us not just me". God then replied in verse 17, "Yes".

To pester God is not a sin if we are acting in faith and not out of greed or vanity. Abraham repeated his request six times before he was satisfied Jacob disobeyed a direct order from God to let him go as the day was breaking, and Moses turned down God's offer to bless just him if He was not willing to bless the Israelites as well. Not on one occasion in the three accounts above do we see or hear God angry. He did not rebuke any of the characters involved in our examples, rather He blessed them and honoured them even more. Notice that in the case of Moses, in verse 18, after God had agreed to his request, Moses put his friendship with God to a harder test by asking to see the face of God; again God honoured Moses's faith but covered his face when He passed by so that Moses saw only God's back parts.

God always honours profound faith because faith is the nature of God. The Bible tells us that the worlds were created by faith in Hebrews, 11:3:

Through faith we understand that the worlds were framed by the word of God, so that things which are seen were not made of things which do appear.

The Bible tells us that God does not lie and that He does not repent from His promises in Numbers, 21:21:

God is not a man, that he should lie; neither the son of man, that he should repent: hath he said, and shall he not do it? Or hath he spoken, and shall he not make it good?

The only way to find out for sure whether God is a liar or not, is by reminding Him of His promises to you. God can neither deny making a promise nor can He back out from executing His parental obligations towards you. He Himself taught us that a man should take care of his own household and we are members of God's own household (1 Timothy 5:8).

But if any provide not for his own, and specially for those of his own house, he hath denied the faith, and is worse than an infidel.

If God fails in His fatherly obligations to me, He has no right to expect me to take care of my own household because I am only following His own example. We know without a shadow of a doubt that God never fails, therefore we need not be afraid when we constantly and relentlessly remind Him of His promises. We need to approach Him respectfully and humbly, but with great assertiveness concerning our covenant rights.

Hannah - 1 Sam 1:9-20

9 So Hannah rose up after they had eaten in Shiloh, and after they had drunk. Now Eli the priest sat upon a seat by a post of the temple of the LORD. 10 And she was in bitterness of soul, and prayed unto the LORD, and wept sore. 11 And she vowed a vow, and said, O LORD of hosts, if thou wilt indeed look on the affliction of thine handmaid, and remember me, and not forget thine handmaid, but wilt give unto thine *handmaid a man child, then I will give him unto the LORD all the days of his life, and there shall no razor come upon his head. **12** And it came to pass, as she continued praying before the LORD, that Eli marked her mouth. **13** Now Hannah, she spake in her heart; only her lips moved, but her voice was not heard: therefore Eli thought she had been drunken. **14** And Eli said unto her, How long wilt thou be drunken? Put away thy wine from thee. **15** And Hannah answered and said, No, my lord, I am a woman of a sorrowful spirit: I have drunk neither wine nor strong drink, but have poured out my soul before the LORD. **16** Count not thine handmaid for a daughter of Belial: for out of the abundance of my complaint and grief have I spoken hitherto. **17** Then Eli answered and said, Go in peace: and the God of Israel grant thee thy petition that thou hast asked of him. **18** And she said, Let thine handmaid find grace in thy sight. So the woman went her way, and did eat, and her countenance was no more sad. **19** And they rose up in the morning early, and worshipped before the LORD, and returned, and came to their house to Ramah: and Elkanah knew Hannah his wife; and the LORD remembered her. **20** Wherefore it came to pass, when the time was come about after Hannah had conceived, that she bare a son, and called his name Samuel, saying, Because I have asked him of the LORD.*

This is a story we are quite familiar with. It is another instance of perseverance in prayer. Hannah, according to verse 7 of the same chapter, had a habit of repeating the same prayer to God yearly. Surely, God must have been fed up with this nuisance of a woman who troubled Him every year for the same petty request. Couldn't she tell that God was not interested in her problems?

Hannah was not put off by the "seeming reluctance" of God to help her, but instead prayed harder and harder. The Bible tells us twice in verses 5 and 6 respectively that God had shut her womb. Hannah did not allow this verdict to deter her from her

23

purpose but prayed the more until she was considered to be drunk by Eli the High priest. Hannah answered and told Eli that she was not drunk, but merely a desperate woman.

Each time Hannah prayed to God, she no doubt reminded God of His promise to the Israelites that they would be fruitful in childbearing.

<u>Exodus 23:26</u>

There shall nothing cast their young, nor be barren, in thy land: the number of thy days I will fulfil.

Not even God could turn down such a compelling argument as this. He was obliged not only to open Hannah's womb, He gave her a son who became the leader of the Israelites for a while and was both a priest and a great prophet of God. It did not end there; Hannah had other children after Samuel, three sons and two daughters.

God does not just honour the specific requests of stubborn people like Abraham, Jacob, Moses and Hannah, He blesses them excessively afterwards. That is what Hebrews, 11:6 is talking about when it says:

But without faith it is impossible to please him: for he that cometh to God must believe that he is, and that he is a rewarder of them that diligently seek him.

If all God does is grant the specific requests of fervent Christians, then there is really no reward. It would merely be a fulfilment of God's promises, but the Bible tells us that God rewards our diligence as well. So God will not just give you that specific thing for which you asked, but will also recognise your persistence and give you something extra that you did not ask for. According to Ephesians 3:20:

Now unto him that is able to do exceeding abundantly above all that we ask or think, according to the power that worketh in us.

So what do you do when a prayer point has not been answered despite your diligence, fasting, praying, giving, tithing, etc? Well the answer is simple; you simply make that another prayer point, which means that you have to ask God why He has not granted your request. You cannot simply just let it go and pretend as if it was nothing. Stop pretending that it was probably not God's will, that you did not have enough faith, or that you probably committed one too many sins. Don't let people easily convince you that it is not God's time yet as this is a convenient way of accepting disappointment.

Daniel prayed to God and expected results. He waited for the time of fulfilment and was sad when it seemed that God had failed. Daniel did not conclude anything and God extended him the courtesy of explaining to Daniel why his prayer request had been delayed:

Daniel 10: 11-13

11 And he said unto me, O Daniel, a man greatly beloved, understand the words that I speak unto thee, and stand upright: for unto thee am I now sent. And when he had spoken this word unto me, I stood trembling. 12 Then said he unto me, Fear not, Daniel: for from the first day that thou didst set thine heart to understand, and to chasten thyself before thy God, thy words were heard, and I am come for thy words. 13 But the prince of the kingdom of Persia withstood me one and twenty days: but, lo, Michael,

25

one of the chief princes, came to help me; and I remained there with the kings of Persia.

The explanation for unanswered prayers or great disappointments in our lives should proceed from God and not men. God sent an angel to offer explanation to Daniel. God will always explain things to us through prayer, waiting on Him, worshipping Him and even day to day events, *if* we are patient and insistent enough. God is obliged to explain to me why He has not granted my request which was properly predicated on His word. God is neither a man that He should lie nor the son of man that He should repent. He will not bully me into keeping quiet if I ask Him to tell me why my prayers to Him have not been answered, He is man enough (or should I say God enough) to kindly comfort me and give me both an explanation and the grace to bear my disappointment. It is only then that I can confidently say that God has not failed me but He has a higher purpose or that His time for fulfilling my request has not yet come.

Never take no for an answer when you have exercised your faith diligently before God. Believe me, if your insistence is respectful and sincere God will neither punish nor kill you for it. Isaiah 45:11 says:

11 Thus saith the LORD, the Holy One of Israel, and his Maker, Ask me of things to come concerning my sons, and concerning the work of my hands command ye me.

This is your licence to respectfully approach God and remind Him of His promises. All you need to say to God is "you said". God, as I have already stated above, cannot deny making a statement if He made it and will not look for excuses for not performing His promises.

Elsewhere in Isaiah 55: 10-11, God explains to us what happens to His word whenever He utters it saying:

10 For as the rain cometh down, and the snow from heaven, and returneth not thither, but watereth the earth, and maketh it bring forth and bud, that it may give seed to the sower, and bread to the eater: 11 So shall my word be that goeth forth out of my mouth: it shall not return unto me void, but it shall accomplish that which I please, and it shall prosper in the thing whereto I sent it.

All you need do is ask God to fulfil His statement in Isaiah 55:10-11, and He will honour His word in your life. The Bible makes it clear that those who know their God will do exploits (Daniel 11:32), the more you know about Him the more you accomplish in prayer. So stop making excuses for God, stop trying to make things easier or patronising Him. Do not allow people to offer explanations to you that do not proceed from God.

Elisha - 2 Kings 4:20-27

20 *And when he had taken him, and brought him to his mother, he sat on her knees till noon, and then died.* **21** *And she went up, and laid him on the bed of the man of God, and shut the door upon him, and went out.* **22** *And she called unto her husband, and said, Send me, I pray thee, one of the young men, and one of the asses, that I may run to the man of God, and come again.* **23** *And he said, Wherefore wilt thou go to him to day? it is neither new moon, nor sabbath. And she said, It shall be well.* **24** *Then she saddled an ass, and said to her servant, Drive, and go forward; slack not thy riding for me, except I bid thee.* **25** *So she went and came unto the man of God to mount Carmel. And it came to pass, when the man of God saw her afar off, that he said to Gehazi his servant, Behold, yonder is that Shunammite:* **26** *Run now, I pray thee, to meet her, and say unto her, Is it well with thee? is it well with thy husband? is it well with the child? And she answered, It is well.* **27** *And when she came to the man of God to the hill, she caught him by the feet: but Gehazi came near to thrust her away. And the man of God said, Let her alone; for her soul is vexed within her: and the LORD hath hid it from me, and hath not told me.*

Elisha had befriended the woman in this account because the woman had ministered to his needs constantly. He had asked God to give her a child and the child had now died. When Elisha became aware of the problem, the Bible tells us that Elisha was surprised because he did not know that the child had died, he in fact admitted that God had hidden it from him. He did not make excuses, he did not act coy and pretend as if it was God's will for the child to die or that it was the woman's sins or lack of faith that was responsible for the child's death.

Elisha did not leave it there though. He refused to take "no" for an answer and this was what followed (2 Kings 4:29-36):

29 Then he said to Gehazi, Gird up thy loins, and take my staff in thine hand, and go thy way: if thou meet any man, salute him not; and if any salute thee, answer him not again: and lay my staff upon the face of the child. 30 And the mother of the child said, As the LORD liveth, and as thy soul liveth, I will not leave thee. And he arose, and followed her. 31 And Gehazi passed on before them, and laid the staff upon the face of the child; but there was neither voice, nor hearing. Wherefore he went again to meet him, and told him, saying, the child is not awaked. 32 And when Elisha was come into the house, behold, the child was dead, and laid upon his bed. 33 He went in therefore, and shut the door upon them twain, and prayed unto the LORD. 34 And he went up, and lay upon the child, and put his mouth upon his mouth, and his eyes upon his eyes, and his hands upon his hands: and he stretched himself upon the child; and the flesh of the child waxed warm. 35 Then he returned, and walked in the house to and fro; and went up, and stretched himself upon him: and the child sneezed seven times, and the child opened his eyes. 36 And he called Gehazi, and said, Call this Shunammite. So he called her. And when she was come in unto him, he said, Take up thy son.

Even though Elisha was not aware of the boy's death, he did not make any assumptions about God's will for the situation; instead he prevailed in prayer. Firstly, Elisha sent Gehazi, his servant, to minister to the dead child but this failed. Elisha could have stopped at that point and given up, but he did not, rather he intensified his efforts by applying physical contact twice before the miracle was complete.

Elisha derived his ministry from his master, Elijah, and inherited a double portion of Elijah's ministerial prowess and anointing. The Bible tells us concerning Elijah that he was not cut from any special cloth nor did he have any special abilities which God did not give him, as a matter of fact, the Bible tells us that Elijah was very much like us (James 5:16-17).

16 *Confess your faults one to another, and pray one for another, that ye may be healed. The effectual fervent prayer of a righteous man availeth much.* **17** *Elias was a man subject to like passions as we are, and he prayed earnestly that it might not rain: and it rained not on the earth by the space of three years and six months.*

Jabez - 1 Chronicles 4:9-10

9 *And Jabez was more honourable than his brethren: and his mother called his name Jabez, saying, Because I bare him with sorrow.* **10** *And Jabez called on the God of Israel, saying, Oh that thou wouldest bless me indeed, and enlarge my coast, and that thine hand might be with me, and that thou wouldest keep me from evil, that it may not grieve me! And God granted him that which he requested.*

Most of us have, at some point or another, prayed the same prayer as Jabez in our personal walk with God. After all, which one of us does not want God to bless him, enlarge his coast, get a helping hand from God, be kept from and not be grieved by evil? It is a strange thing though that it seems that very few of us tend to get the same result as Jabez.

The inclusion of Jabez's short history in 1 Chronicles 4: 9-10 is a curious thing as the account is totally disjointed and out of both context and sequence. Who really was Jabez? All we know of him is that he was born out of sorrow and thus was aptly named, he became more honourable than his brethren and he prayed to God. It is evident from this sequence that Jabez was already more honourable than his brethren before God blessed him. Could this be an instructive indication of why God blessed him? Could it be that, like Cornelius and Rahab, he was a God-fearing man even before he had full knowledge of God? Could it be that, regardless of Jabez's obvious sorrowful circumstances in

30

life, he dared to have faith in God who is the justifier of men? Was his faith in God counted for righteousness as with Abraham?

There are too many questions that come to mind about Jabez, but one thing is clear, God honoured his prayer and singled him out in his generation.

A lot of us have lived lives of obscurity without any significant events or meaningful influences. Nobody it would appear really cares about us because of the circumstances of our birth, our lineage, our physical appearance, our parent's poverty etc. We may even have resigned ourselves to our fate and given up on ever achieving greatness or renown. Being born again for us only means that we have a sanctuary to hide in and continue our seemingly meaningless existence. We will die the same way we lived: unloved, unwanted, unrecognised, untalented and insignificant.

Jabez refused to accept the verdict over his life which was dictated by the very meaning of his name. He refused to accept the fact that the circumstances of his birth were sorrowful, he refused to resign himself to his obvious destiny; instead he rose above his circumstances and cried earnestly to God until he was granted his request.

The God of Jabez is still looking for honourable men and women in every generation. If you dare to believe in Him like Jabez did, though your life may mean nothing to you or indeed anyone else, He will do what He did with Jabez for you. He will make you more honourable than your brethren and record your name in a significant place in the annals of history so get on your knees and begin to prevail in prayer. Do not be put off if it appears that your blessing is delayed, cry to God the more, (weep if you must), complain, moan, repeat yourself over and over again, but, most importantly, remind God of His word concerning that request because He cannot deny His own words.

<u>Hezekiah - Isaiah 38 1:8</u>

1 In those days was Hezekiah sick unto death. And Isaiah the prophet the son of Amoz came unto him, and said unto him, Thus saith the LORD, Set thine house in order: for thou shalt die, and not live. 2 Then Hezekiah turned his face toward the wall, and prayed unto the LORD, 3 And said, Remember now, O LORD, I beseech thee, how I have walked before thee in truth and with a perfect heart, and have done that which is good in thy sight. And Hezekiah wept sore. 4 Then came the word of the LORD to Isaiah, saying, 5 Go, and say to Hezekiah, Thus saith the LORD, the God of David thy father, I have heard thy prayer, I have seen thy tears: behold, I will add unto thy days fifteen years. 6 And I will deliver thee and this city out of the hand of the king of Assyria: and I will defend this city. 7 And this shall be a sign unto thee from the LORD, that the LORD will do this thing that he hath spoken; 8 Behold, I will bring again the shadow of the degrees, which is gone down in the sun dial of Ahaz, ten degrees backward. So the sun returned ten degrees, by which degrees it was gone down.

Isaiah the great prophet of God had just pronounced a death sentence on Hezekiah, the King. The pronouncement did not emanate from Isaiah but was in fact a prophetical statement from God Himself which Hezekiah ordinarily ought to have been bound by. Hezekiah rejected this pronouncement and instead pleaded with God fervently to spare his life. God was reminded of how Hezekiah had served Him faithfully. God was obliged to reverse the sentence over Hezekiah's life and extended his lifespan miraculously. In order to demonstrate His

32

commitment to Hezekiah's request, God actually altered the normal course of nature.

Chapter 2

Accepting Status Quo

The common theme with the examples above is that the people involved simply refused to accept the status quo. They refused to be bound by the dictates of their circumstances, the laws of nature, the opinion of men and even dared to challenge God's disposition towards their position.

There are people in the Bible who decided not to change their circumstances and simply gave up. The example that readily comes to mind is that of Eli, the High Priest of God. God used Samuel to warn Eli of what was to become of his children as a result of their sins and blatant disregard for God. Eli was unperturbed by this and simply accepted the situation (1 Samuel 3:12-18).

12 In that day I will perform against Eli all things which I have spoken concerning his house: when I begin, I will also make an end. 13 For I have told him that I will judge his house for ever for the iniquity which he knoweth; because his sons made themselves vile, and he restrained them not. 14 And therefore I have sworn unto the house of Eli, that the iniquity of Eli's house shall not be purged with sacrifice nor offering for ever. 15 And Samuel lay until the morning, and opened the doors of the house of the LORD. And Samuel feared to shew Eli the vision. 16 Then Eli called Samuel, and said, Samuel, my son. And he answered, Here am I. 17 And he said, What is the thing that the LORD hath said unto thee? I pray thee *hide it not from me: God do so to thee, and more also, if thou hide any thing from me of all the things that he said unto thee. **18** And Samuel told him every whit, and hid nothing from him. And he said, It is the LORD: let him do what seemeth him good.*

Let's not forget who Eli was; he was the High Priest who prophesied to Hannah (in our example above) that she would conceive and give birth to Samuel. He had been used of God in the past and was still, as far as we can tell from the scriptures, a good man. Eli's response to God's warning, however, belies his great stature as a man of God. He acted without faith or care. He simply accepted the verdict that God was going to destroy his entire lineage. He could have approached God respectfully and supplicated before Him and ask for forgiveness for at least his own lapses in bringing up his children badly. God cannot be put in a box so we cannot conclude that God could not have reversed the judgement or at least mitigated it somewhat. Hezekiah was unlike Eli; he dared to challenge God's judgement and prevailed, just like Moses, his ancestor, had interceded for the Israelites hundreds of years before him.

The story of Eli is very sad because God proceeded to execute His fierce judgement as stated by Samuel. The story reminds us of the story of the twelve spies sent to survey the promised land before eventual possession.

<u>Joshua and Caleb – Numbers 13:26-32 & 14:30</u>

26 *And they went and came to Moses, and to Aaron, and to all the congregation of the children of Israel, unto the wilderness of Paran, to Kadesh; and brought back word unto them, and unto all the congregation, and shewed them the fruit of the land. **27** And they told him, and said, We came unto the land whither thou sentest us, and surely it floweth with milk* *and honey; and this is the fruit of it.* **28** *Nevertheless the people be strong that dwell in the land, and the cities are walled, and very great: and moreover we saw the children of Anak there.* **29** *The Amalekites dwell in the land of the south: and the Hittites, and the Jebusites, and the Amorites, dwell in the mountains: and the Canaanites dwell by the sea, and by the coast of Jordan.* **30** *And Caleb stilled the people before Moses, and said, Let us go up at once, and possess it; for we are well able to overcome it.* **31** *But the men that went up with him said, We be not able to go up against the people; for they are stronger than we.* **32** *And they brought up an evil report of the land which they had searched unto the children of Israel, saying, The land, through which we have gone to search it, is a land that eateth up the inhabitants thereof; and all the people that we saw in it are men of a great stature.*

Ten out the twelve spies sent out to survey the land came back with an evil report, thereby negating the divine ability of God to perform what he had promised. These men undermined God greatly and almost led the people to rebellion against God and Moses. In His anger, God cursed them and spared only Joshua and Caleb who, though they saw the same things as the other ten men came back with a positive report which was predicated on God's ability as opposed to human strength. They refused to accept the fact that the giants in the land would prevent them from inheriting it. Joshua and Caleb never denied the fact that there were indeed giants in the land as this was a true fact; instead they saw the giants as insignificant compared with the greatness of Yahweh, the all sufficient one. As a result, God blessed both men and allowed them to survive the wilderness journey. Joshua was promoted to leader in place of Moses, and Caleb was given an entire mountain home (Joshua 14:6-13)

Chapter 3

Negative insistence

Sometimes people insist on their request in a negative sense. This sort of insistence can be displayed either in the form of greed or doubt. Greed can be manifested when people desire something of God simply because they want more; in such cases their motives are always wrong. Sometimes greed manifests itself in our requests to God because we are covetous; we simply want to be like others.

Doubting God will sometimes prompt us to ask Him to do things to prove Himself to us before we can trust Him. The shocking thing is that sometimes, even when our requests are predicated on either greed or doubt, God still obliges our faithless requests. Let us consider a few examples from the Bible in no particular order.

The Israelites desired food – Exodus 16:3-13

3 And the children of Israel said unto them, Would to God we had died by the hand of the LORD in the land of Egypt, when we sat by the flesh pots, and when we did eat bread to the full; for ye have brought us forth into this wilderness, to kill this whole assembly with hunger. 4 Then said the LORD unto Moses, Behold, I will rain bread from heaven for you; and the people shall go out and gather a certain rate every day, that I may prove them, whether they will walk in my law, or no. 5 And it shall come to pass, that on the sixth day they shall prepare that which they bring in; and it shall be twice as much as they gather daily. 6 And Moses and Aaron said unto all the children of Israel, At even, then ye shall know that the LORD hath brought you out from the land of Egypt: 7 And in the morning, then ye shall see the glory of the LORD; for that he heareth your murmurings against the LORD: and what are we, that ye murmur against us? 8 And Moses said, This shall be, when the LORD shall give you in the evening flesh to eat, and in the morning bread to the full; for that the LORD heareth your murmurings which ye murmur against him: and what are we? your murmurings are not against us, but against the LORD. 9 And Moses spake unto Aaron, Say unto all the congregation of the children of Israel, Come near before the LORD: for he hath heard your murmurings. 10 And it came to pass, as Aaron spake unto the whole congregation of the children of Israel, that they looked toward the wilderness, and, behold, the glory of the LORD appeared in the cloud. 11 And the LORD spake unto Moses, saying, 12 I have heard the murmurings of the children of Israel: speak unto them, saying, At even ye shall eat flesh, and in the morning ye shall be filled with bread; and ye shall know that I am the LORD your God.13 And it came to pass, that at even the quails came up, and covered the camp: and in the morning the dew lay round about the host.

This is a classic example of how not to insist on the performance of our requests. God proactively and voluntarily rescued the Israelites from 400 years of slavery. The whole process of their deliverance was miraculous as God performed great acts to exert His majesty over Pharaoh before the latter let the Israelites go. Shortly after their rescue, the Israelites, God's chosen people, accused Him of bringing them into the wilderness to starve them to death and demanded food in a very negative way. They threw God's sacrifice back in His face by stating that they preferred the lifestyle of slavery they had in Egypt to what God had in store for them. God was obliged to prove His awesomeness to these ingrates and complainers, as seen above. However there was a consequence for this as God's gift to them later became a snare.

Psalm 78 verses 19 – 31 (below) relates the consequence of prayer motivated by doubt and lust. I pray that God will not answer any of our negative prayers even if we tempt Him sore as the Israelites did. We need to always examine our hearts and motivation to ascertain why we are insisting on certain blessings from God.

19 Yea, they spake against God; they said, Can God furnish a table in the wilderness? 20 Behold, he smote the rock, that the waters gushed out, and the streams overflowed; can he give bread also? can he provide flesh for his people? 21 Therefore the LORD heard this, and was wroth: so a fire was kindled against Jacob, and anger also came up against Israel; 22 Because they believed not in God, and trusted not in his salvation: 23 Though he had commanded the clouds from above, and opened the doors of heaven, 24 And had rained down manna upon them to eat, and had given them of the corn of heaven. 25 Man did eat angels' food: he sent them meat to the full. 26 He caused an east wind to blow in the heaven: and by his power he brought in the south wind. 27 He rained flesh also upon them as dust, and feathered fowls like as the sand of the sea: 28 And he let it fall in the midst of their camp, round about their habitations. 29 So they did eat, and were well filled: for he gave them their own desire; 30 They were not estranged from their lust. But while their meat was yet in their mouths, 31 The wrath of God came upon them, and slew the fattest of them, and smote down the chosen men of Israel.

The Israelites demand a King – 1 Samuel 8: 4-7

4 Then all the elders of Israel gathered themselves together, and came to Samuel unto Ramah, 5 And said unto him, Behold, thou art old, and thy sons walk not in thy ways: now make us a king to judge us like all the nations. 6 But the thing displeased Samuel, when they said, Give us a king to judge us. And Samuel prayed unto the LORD. 7 And the LORD said unto Samuel, Hearken unto the voice of the people in all that they say unto thee: for they have not rejected thee, but they have rejected me, that I should not reign over them.

The Israelites rejected the reign of God simply because they wanted to be like other nations. They had forgotten the promises God made to their forbear, Abraham, Isaac and Jacob that He would be their God and make them a unique race. They preferred to follow the lust in their hearts and were ruled by covetousness instead. Again, God could have rejected their request, He could have punished them and remained their God, but rather He granted their negative request to demonstrate the foolishness of men's wisdom to future generations like ours.

A detailed study of the records of the Kings of Israel as contained in 1 Samuel – 2 Chronicles will show that only Kings like David, Hezekiah, Jehosaphat and a few others really led the Israelites rightly. The Israelites ended up in captivity from which God had earlier rescued them because of their bad leadership. It was Jehovah who kept intervening from time to time to prevent the total annihilation of the Jews even though they had rejected Him up until the time of Adolph Hiltler and even currently in the Middle East. They should never have rejected Him as King.

<u>Thomas the doubter, John 20: 24-29</u>

24 But Thomas, one of the twelve, called Didymus, was not with them when Jesus came. 25 The other disciples therefore said unto him, We have seen the Lord. But he said unto them, Except I shall see in his hands the print of the nails, and put my finger into the print of the nails, and thrust my hand into his side, I will not believe. 26 And after eight days again his disciples were within, and Thomas with them: then came Jesus, the doors being shut, and stood in the midst, and said, Peace be unto you. 27 Then saith he to Thomas, Reach hither thy finger, and behold my hands; and reach hither thy hand, and thrust it into my side: and be not faithless, but believing. 28 And Thomas answered and said unto him, My Lord and my God. 29 Jesus saith unto him, Thomas, because thou hast seen me, thou hast believed: blessed are they that have not seen, and yet have believed.

The story of doubting Thomas was first told to me when I was in Sunday school as a pre-teen and all through my life it has served as a reminder to me of the need to trust God for who He is and not what I make of Him. It is very convenient to mock Thomas and make him a bad example, but are we all really any different to him? In Thomas's defence, at least he was sincere about his need to see the resurrected Jesus; there was no ulterior personal gain for him in the request – he simply wanted to experience what the others had experienced. But the Lord's rebuke remains very valid; we need to trust God more.

The Lord again decided to honour the prayer of a faithless man to teach a valuable lesson to future generations of believers. Thomas was not different from the Jews who demanded a sign of deity from Jesus in Matthew 12: 39-42.

39 But he answered and said unto them, An evil and adulterous generation seeketh after a sign; and there shall no sign be given to it, but the *sign of the prophet Jonas: **40** For as Jonas was three days and three nights in the whale's belly; so shall the Son of man be three days and three nights in the heart of the earth. **41** The men of Nineveh shall rise in judgment with this generation, and shall condemn it: because they repented at the preaching of Jonas; and, behold, a greater than Jonas is here. **42** The queen of the south shall rise up in the judgment with this generation, and shall condemn it: for she came from the uttermost parts of the earth to hear the wisdom of Solomon; and, behold, a greater than Solomon is here.*

Sometimes we may want to validate our faith in God via signs did as Gideon in Judges 6: 33-40:

*Then all the Midianites and the Amalekites and the children of the east were gathered together, and went over, and pitched in the valley of Jezreel. **34** But the Spirit of the LORD came upon Gideon, and he blew a trumpet; and Abiezer was gathered after him. **35** And he sent messengers throughout all Manasseh; who also was gathered after him: and he sent messengers unto Asher, and unto Zebulun, and unto Naphtali; and they came up to meet them. **36** And Gideon said unto God, If thou wilt save Israel by mine hand, as thou hast said. **37** Behold, I will put a fleece of wool in the floor; and if the dew be on the fleece only, and it be dry upon all the earth beside, then shall I know that thou wilt save Israel by mine hand, as thou hast said. **38** And it was so: for he rose up early on the morrow, and thrust the fleece together, and wringed the dew out of the fleece, a bowl full of water. **39** And Gideon said unto God, Let not thine anger be hot against me, and I will speak but this once: let me prove, I pray thee, but this once with the fleece; let it now be dry only upon the fleece, and upon all the ground let there be dew. **40** And God did so that night: for it was dry upon the fleece only, and there was dew on all the ground.*

However, we should not make a habit of it. Gideon has been criticised profusely by many christians, but I believe he may be excused simply because at the time of his call by Yahweh,

Gideon had not previously experienced the majesty of God. He had lived a relatively insignificant life hiding always from enemies, hence he objected to being called a mighty man of valour. It was therefore a big leap in faith for him to do what God asked. Notice that God did not chastise him for this as He did the Israelites, Thomas and Zachariah, the father of John the Baptist.

Zachariah – Luke 1: 5-20

5 There was in the days of Herod, the king of Judaea, a certain priest named Zacharias, of the course of Abia: and his wife was of the daughters of Aaron, and her name was Elisabeth. 6 And they were both righteous before God, walking in all the commandments and ordinances of the Lord blameless. 7 And they had no child, because that Elisabeth was barren, and they both were now well stricken in years. 8 And it came to pass, that while he executed the priest's office before God in the order of his course, 9 According to the custom of the priest's office, his lot was to burn incense when he went into the temple of the Lord. 10 And the whole multitude of the people were praying without at the time of incense. 11 And there appeared unto him an angel of the Lord standing on the right side of the altar of incense. 12 And when Zacharias saw him, he was troubled, and fear fell upon him. 13 But the angel said unto him, Fear not, Zacharias: for thy prayer is heard; and thy wife Elisabeth shall bear thee a son, and thou shalt call his name John. 14 And thou shalt have joy and gladness; and many shall rejoice at his birth. 15 For he shall be great in the sight of the Lord, and shall drink neither wine nor strong drink; and he shall be filled with the Holy Ghost, even from his mother's womb. 16 And many of the children of Israel shall he turn to the Lord their God. 17 And he shall go before him in the spirit and power of Elias, to turn the hearts of the fathers to the children, and the disobedient to the wisdom of the just; to make ready a people prepared for the Lord. 18 And Zacharias said unto the angel, Whereby shall I know this? for I am an old man, and my wife well stricken in years.

19 And the angel answering said unto him, I am Gabriel, that stand in the presence of God; and am sent to speak unto thee, and to shew thee these glad tidings. 20 And, behold, thou shalt be dumb, and not able to speak, until the day that these things shall be performed, because thou believest not my words, which shall be fulfilled in their season.

The main difference between Gideon and Zachariah is that unlike Gideon, Zachariah was a priest, a man of good report who had walked with God for a long time. It is inexcusable for someone of his calibre and credentials to make such a faithless and irresponsible request of God (please read verses 6-7 of Like, Chapter 1 above to see Zachariah's profile). The more we know God, the more our faith in Him should grow.

The same angel appeared to Mary, the mother of our Lord Jesus Christ, with a similar message. Please note the difference in the responses to the word of God. Luke 1: Verse 38.

And Mary said, Behold the handmaid of the Lord; be it unto me according to thy word. And the angel departed from her.

The reason I am stressing this point of negative insistence is because I want to differentiate between it and legitimate and genuine insistence in prayer. Please note that neither Gideon nor Zachariah did the right thing. I am not justifying the attitude of Gideon; rather I only attempted to mitigate the implications of his actions by referring to his ignorance of God's ability.

Negative insistence is never to be classified as prevailing prayer; it is motivated by doubt, greed and total disrespect for God. Had God refused to honour Gideon and the latter continued to insist on the performance of his request, I am convinced that Gideon would have been faced with divine punishment for disobedience.

Insisting on negative things to test God's ability can only lead to rebellion, as the more God refuses the request, the more we tend to doubt His ability. This leads to dissatisfaction, murmuring and ultimately rebellion, and we know that according to Hebrew 12; 28-29;

28 Wherefore we receiving a kingdom which cannot be moved, let us have grace, whereby we may serve God acceptably with reverence and godly fear: 29 For our God is a consuming fire.

Chapter 4

When God says "NO"

I have heard people stating that God never says "no" to prayers and frankly I strongly disagree. God does say "no" to certain prayer points or requests, even when they emanate from a sincere heart. It is pointless trying to ascertain accurately why God refuses to grant certain requests as He only reveals things to us as it pleases Him. If God decides to say "no" categorically to our requests, though they are predicated on faith, compassion, love and sincerity, what then do we do?

The answer to this question is answered in the Bible. If God firmly rejects a prayer point or request, the best course of action is to accept His decision and trust Him; because He knows the beginning from the end. He no doubt has a valid reason for saying "no".

Let us now consider some examples from the Bible to illustrate how to accept when God's says "no" to our requests. By the way, the examples below are of good men who had a sincere desire to partake of God's plan but yet were refused. This only demonstrates the sovereignty of God over our lives.

23 And I besought the LORD at that time, saying, 24 O LORD God, thou hast begun to shew thy servant thy greatness, and thy mighty hand: for what God is there in heaven or in earth, that can do according to thy works, and according to thy might? 25 I pray thee, let me go over, and see the good land that is beyond Jordan, that goodly mountain, and Lebanon. 26 But the LORD was wroth with me for your sakes, and would not hear me: and the LORD said unto me, Let it suffice thee; speak no more unto me of this matter.

Moses was undergoing divine punishment at the time he asked God to allow him entry into Canaan but was refused. The background to this event is contained in the book of Number 20: 7-12.

7 And the LORD spake unto Moses, saying, 8 Take the rod, and gather thou the assembly together, thou, and Aaron thy brother, and speak ye unto the rock before their eyes; and it shall give forth his water, and thou shalt bring forth to them water out of the rock: so thou shalt give the congregation and their beasts drink. 9 And Moses took the rod from before the LORD, as he commanded him. 10 And Moses and Aaron gathered the congregation together before the rock, and he said unto them, Hear now, ye rebels; must we fetch you water out of this rock? 11 And Moses lifted up his hand, and with his rod he smote the rock twice: and the water came out abundantly, and the congregation drank, and their beasts also. 12 And the LORD spake unto Moses and Aaron, Because ye believed me not, to sanctify me in the eyes of the children of Israel, therefore ye shall not bring this congregation into the land which I have given them.

Moses had allowed some time to pass from the time God judged him for his lack of reverence before asking for leniency,

47

but we see here that God had made up His mind that Moses would not enter the Promised Land and He kept that resolve.

Whenever I recall that event you must believe me, I actually feel a slight tremor running down my body. It is a scary thing that God can be so severe with even such a man as Moses whom He had used so mightily. God attested to Moses's credentials in the following passages:

Numbers 12:3

(Now the man Moses was very meek, above all the men which were upon the face of the earth.)

Deuteronomy 34: 5-12

5 So Moses the servant of the LORD died there in the land of Moab, according to the word of the LORD. 6 And he buried him in a valley in the land of Moab, over against Bethpeor: but no man knoweth of his sepulchre unto this day. 7 And Moses was an hundred and twenty years old when he died: his eye was not dim, nor his natural force abated. 8 And the children of Israel wept for Moses in the plains of Moab thirty days: so the days of weeping and mourning for Moses were ended. 9 And Joshua the son of Nun was full of the spirit of wisdom; for Moses had laid his hands upon him: and the children of Israel hearkened unto him, and did as the LORD commanded Moses. 10 And there arose not a prophet since in Israel like unto Moses, whom the LORD knew face to face, 11 In all the signs and the wonders, which the LORD sent him to do in the land of Egypt to Pharaoh, and to all his servants, and to all his land, 12 And in all that mighty hand, and in all the great terror which Moses shewed in the sight of all Israel.

Moses was a unique man in his generation and was revered by even his enemies. He was the only man that God personally held a funeral service for. God kept the burial place of Moses secret because had the location been known, people of Canaan would have attempted to deify him. Even the Devil contested for the body of Moses;

Jude verse 9

Yet Michael the archangel, when contending with the devil he disputed about the body of Moses, durst not bring against him a railing accusation, but said, The Lord rebuke thee.

Despite all of Moses's achievement and greatness, God still said "no" to him. Maybe now you can understand why a wretched man like me would be so afraid to displease the living God; what would my punishment be?

Samuel mourns for Saul 1 Samuel 16:1

And the LORD said unto Samuel, How long wilt thou mourn for Saul, seeing I have rejected him from reigning over Israel? fill thine horn with oil, and go, I will send thee to Jesse the Bethlehemite: for I have provided me a king among his sons.

Though God had rejected Saul, the first king of Israel, Samuel was still mourning for him. He had probably approached God prayerfully in intercession to no avail. God's word to Samuel was final. "I have rejected Saul, end of story".

God followed this with clear instructions as to how Samuel was to go about appointing the next king. This simply means that as far as God was concerned, Saul was ancient history and God was going to get on with things and make alternative arrangements for the kingdom of Israel.

I pray that God will not be dismissive concerning us; I pray that I pray that God will never pass us by, and move on to somebody else, just because of our sins. It is truly a terrible thing to fall into the hands of the living God.

Samuel did not bother to argue with God after this statement; he simply accepted God's wishes and went about the business of seeking the son of Jesse out.

David and the temple 1 Chronicles 2-5

2 Then David the king stood up upon his feet, and said, Hear me, my brethren, and my people: As for me, I had in mine heart to build an house of rest for the ark of the covenant of the LORD, and for the footstool of our God, and had made ready for the building: 3 But God said unto me, Thou shalt not build an house for my name, because thou hast been a man of war, and hast shed blood. 4 Howbeit the LORD God of Israel chose me before all the house of my father to be king over Israel for ever: for he hath chosen Judah to be the ruler; and of the house of Judah, the house of my father; and among the sons of my father he liked me to make me king over all Israel: 5 And of all my sons, (for the LORD hath given me many sons,) he hath chosen Solomon my son to sit upon the throne of the kingdom of the LORD over Israel. 6 And he said unto me, Solomon thy son, he shall build my house and my courts: for I have chosen him to be my son, and I will be his father.

David loved his God so much that he wanted to build Him a house of worship. He approached God with his desire but was rejected. God had other plans in place and He told David why he was being refused.

Sometimes God may elect to explain Himself and sometimes He may choose not to. He is God and there is nothing we can do about it. In the example of Paul below, again we see God choosing to explain to a man why his prayer was being rejected.

David accepted God's will here, as he did when God decided not to spare the child that was born to Him out of adultery. 2 Samuel 12: 13-23.

13 And David said unto Nathan, I have sinned against the LORD. And Nathan said unto David, The LORD also hath put away thy sin; thou shalt not die. 14 Howbeit, because by this deed thou hast given great occasion to the enemies of the LORD to blaspheme, the child also that is born unto thee shall surely die. 15 And Nathan departed unto his house. And the LORD struck the child that Uriah's wife bare unto David, and it was very sick. 16 David therefore besought God for the child; and David fasted, and went in, and lay all night upon the earth. 17 And the elders of his house arose, and went to him, to raise him up from the earth: but he would not, neither did he eat bread with them. 18 And it came to pass on the seventh day, that the child died. And the servants of David feared to tell him that the child was dead: for they said, Behold, while the child was yet alive, we spake unto him, and he would not hearken unto our voice: how will he then vex himself, if we tell him that the child is dead? 19 But when David saw that his servants whispered, David perceived that the child was dead: therefore David said unto his servants, Is the child dead? And they said, He is dead. 20 Then David arose from the earth, and washed, and anointed himself, and changed his apparel, and came into the house of the LORD, and worshipped: then he came to his own house; and when he required, they set bread before him, and he did eat. 21 Then said his servants unto him, What thing is this that thou hast done? thou didst fast and weep for the child, while it was alive; but when the child was dead, thou didst rise and eat bread. 22 And he said, While the child was yet alive, I fasted and wept: for I said, Who can tell whether GOD will be gracious to me, that the child may live? 23 But now he is dead, wherefore should I fast? can I bring him back again? I shall go to him, but he shall not return to me.

David prayed for the life of the child and humbled himself in his usual manner to no avail; God went ahead with His purpose. The cruelty or otherwise of God is not subject to debate on the matter as He is the potter and we are the clay.

Paul and his thorn in the flesh 2 Corinthians 12:6-9

6 For though I would desire to glory, I shall not be a fool; for I will say the truth: but now I forbear, lest any man should think of me above that which he seeth me to be, or that he heareth of me. 7 And lest I should be exalted above measure through the abundance of the revelations, there was given to me a thorn in the flesh, the messenger of Satan to buffet me, lest I should be exalted above measure. 8 For this thing I besought the Lord thrice, that it might depart from me. 9 And he said unto me, My grace is sufficient for thee: for my strength is made perfect in weakness. Most gladly therefore will I rather glory in my infirmities, that the power of Christ may rest upon me.

Paul, without any doubt, was probably the most celebrated apostle in the Bible, but he was a man nonetheless. He had weaknesses and was probably as susceptible to pride as the rest of us. In order to ensure that Paul was under spiritual discipline God, in His wisdom, installed a weakness in him; a reminder of his frailty and mortality. It is pointless to debate what the weakness was, as there are different opinions on this subject; suffice it to say though that the weakness kept him in check.

The moral of the four examples above is that sometimes even when we persevere in fervent prayer, God may still reject our prayer. The best approach, as we can see from the examples of great men above, is to reverently let go of such requests and wait for His will to be performed in our lives.

Chapter 5

The Story So Far

To quickly recap, so far we have discussed the following;

1. Persistence in prayer. Here we considered the experiences of people like Abraham, Jacob and Moses etc.

2. Not taking "no" for an answer.

3. Negative examples of insistence

4. When God says "no".

The obvious question on your mind at this stage might be why is it so difficult to obtain mercies from God. Why doesn't He just give us what we ask for when we ask for it? Why the need to be insistent and repetitive when we can just ask once and get immediate results? The only answer I have is that God is wiser than us; He knows what is best for us and would not deliberately withhold anything good from us just to punish us or to satisfy Himself by watching us suffer.

The Bible says that if it is in your power to help your brother, do not say to him 'go and come back again', you are expected to help immediately. If God enjoins mere mortals to be prompt and ready to help others, for a stronger reason, I suppose He Himself would adhere to a higher standard.

<u>Proverbs 3:27-28</u>

27 Withhold not good from them to whom it is due, when it is in the power of thine hand to do it. 28 Say not unto thy neighbour, Go, and come again, and to morrow I will give; when thou hast it by thee.

The Bible says, (ask and you shall receive, seek and you shall find, knock and it shall be opened unto you). If you ask your friend for something, if he is truly a friend and is in possession of that thing, would he not help? If you lost something valuable and had to search for it, would it not take some time to locate it and if you knocked on the door and someone was within, would it not be open to you albeit it after a momentary lapse?

God is not a sadist who enjoys needless suffering, He is not a man who is incapable of fulfilling His promises, and He certainly is not accountable to you for how He wants to be approached in prayer. I believe that God is very much interested in building our character through patient dependence on Him. The Bible tells us that the effectual fervent prayer of a righteous man avails much. The Bible also tells us that God is a rewarder of them that diligently seek Him. Stop asking God why He has set the standards for answered prayer and start following the rules.

I know for a fact that sometimes God will provide instant answers to certain prayers and sometimes He may defer the answer because He is in the process of educating you; sometimes there are factors that you may be unaware of which may impact upon the waiting time. In Daniel's case, he had to wait for twenty-one days for his answer, even though God had already answered his prayer on the first day. The delay was due to a spiritual battle in the realm of angels between Angel Gabriel and Satan himself.

<u>Daniel Chapter 10 verses 11-13</u>

11 And he said unto me, O Daniel, a man greatly beloved, understand the words that I speak unto thee, and stand upright: for unto thee am I now sent. And when he had spoken this word unto me, I stood trembling. 12 Then said he unto me, Fear not, Daniel: for from the first day that thou didst set thine heart to understand, and to chasten thyself before thy God, thy words were heard, and I am come for thy words. 13 But the prince of the kingdom of Persia withstood me one and twenty days: but, lo, Michael, one of the chief princes, came to help me; and I remained there with the kings of Persia.

Sometimes God holds back because to put it frankly we are ungrateful children who only ever spend time in prayer to ask for favours and never give thanks to God and appreciate Him for the things He has done.

God wants His children to "grow up" and not "go up". Anybody can climb the stairs to get to the next level, but growing up is a painstaking exercise which demands long-suffering and trusting in God. King Saul climbed up but David grew up.

By far the most common reason for seemingly unanswered prayer is sin. The Bible tells us in Hebrews, Chapter 12, to lay aside every weight of sin which may hinder us in prayer or break our fellowship with God. So if you are living in sin, God may refuse to answer your prayers. Please bear in mind that it is not just things such as fornication or lying that qualify as sin; you may be a selfish person who never gives to anybody, this will still qualify as sin, you may be expected by God to be involved in a certain work, but you are not – this is disobedience, and thus sin.

<u>Isaiah Chapter 59 verses 1-8</u>

1 Behold, the LORD'S hand is not shortened, that it cannot save; neither his ear heavy, that it cannot hear: 2 But your iniquities have separated between you and your God, and your sins have hid his face from you, that he will not hear. 3 For your hands are defiled with blood, and your fingers with iniquity; your lips have spoken lies, your tongue hath muttered perverseness. 4 None calleth for justice, nor any pleadeth for truth: they trust in vanity, and speak lies; they conceive mischief, and bring forth iniquity. 5 They hatch cockatrice' eggs, and weave the spider's web: he that eateth of their eggs dieth, and that which is crushed breaketh out into a viper. 6 Their webs shall not become garments, neither shall they cover themselves with their works: their works are works of iniquity, and the act of violence is in their hands. 7 Their feet run to evil, and they make haste to shed innocent blood: their thoughts are thoughts of iniquity; wasting and destruction are in their paths. 8 The way of peace they know not; and there is no judgment in their goings: they have made them crooked paths: whosoever goeth therein shall not know peace.

I will not elaborate further on this issue. Stop sinning and start getting.

Chapter 6

What Now?

At this stage, I would like to challenge you to shake yourself loose of your misconceptions about God in relation to prayer. God is neither a liar, nor a cheat or a bully who demands worship and praise but is lacking in blessings. He created the entire universe and is still in the business of answering sincere prayers.

Practical follow-up steps

So what happens to me now? You may wish to ask. Like Apostle Paul, I implore you by the mercies of God to humour me and follow the next step; which is a week-long programme of fasting and prayer. I assure you that God will restore to you all the years you may have lost in prayer and endless lists of unanswered prayers that you may have.

I want you to take a week out in fasting and prayer. Please attempt to fast from dawn till dusk (roughly 06:00 – 18:00 hours) and only have one light meal when you break. Please spend at least three conscious hours (which may be scattered) in prayer each day in addition to praying in the Spirit. I would advise you to abstain from any sexual activity during this period if you are married. Set your alarm clock, or discipline yourself to wake up just before dawn and start the day in God's presence.

Day 1

Psalm 100 verse 4

Enter into his gates with thanksgiving, and into his courts with praise: be thankful unto him, and bless his name.

Psalm 105 verses 1-5

1 Bless the LORD, O my soul: and all that is within me, bless his holy name. 2 Bless the LORD, O my soul, and forget not all his benefits: 3 Who forgiveth all thine iniquities; who healeth all thy diseases; 4 Who redeemeth thy life from destruction; who crowneth thee with lovingkindness and tender mercies; 5 Who satisfieth thy mouth with good things; so that thy youth is renewed like the eagle's.

Approach God respectfully, examining yourself and enter His presence firstly with thanksgiving for all the wonderful things He has done for you, your family and friends. This is not a rushed exercise and may take several hours over the course of the day. You should recount as much as you can of God's blessings in your life ever since you gave your life to Him.

Begin with your earliest memories of His involvement in your life up until the present time. No blessing is too small even if it seems repetitive to you. Sing songs of thanksgiving throughout the day and refrain from asking God for any favours. Go to bed early thereby avoiding television as much as possible or other distractions. Study the Psalms which focus on thanksgiving and meditate on your bed consciously as you fall asleep.

Day 2

<u>Psalm 100 verse 4</u>

Enter into his gates with thanksgiving, and into his courts with praise: be thankful unto him, and bless his name.

<u>Psalm 105 verses 1-5</u>

1 Bless the LORD, O my soul: and all that is within me, bless his holy name. 2 Bless the LORD, O my soul, and forget not all his benefits: 3 Who forgiveth all thine iniquities; who healeth all thy diseases; 4 Who redeemeth thy life from destruction; who crowneth thee with lovingkindness and tender mercies; 5 Who satisfieth thy mouth with good things; so that thy youth is renewed like the eagle's.

Start your day again in God's presence and greet Him with praise. Continually praise and magnify Him throughout the day. Consider the world, the universe around you, and everything God has made. Reflect on the biblical testimonies about His works, consider the Jehovah names such as Rapha (the healer), Shalom (peace-giver), Shammar (ever present one), Rohi (the shepherd), Nissi (our banner) etc. Tell Him how great you believe Him to be. Sing songs of praise throughout the day and again study the bible and, sleep early, reflecting on His greatness.

Day 3

This is the day of worship, a day of intense soberness and submission to the awesomeness of God. If you are employed, I would suggest that you take the day off as you cannot afford to be distracted on this day. If you have been following the programme so far, your appetite for food should be waning by now and you may find yourself experiencing a wave of calmness, you may feel quite emotional and vulnerable at this stage.

This is because your body is now under total subjection as it has been deprived of food, sex and entertainment, thus giving free rein to your inner man. If you can, please adopt a kneeling or prostrate posture before the almighty and extol His holy name.

I advise again that you study the book of Psalms focussing on worship. If possible reduce physical communication by remaining indoors throughout the day. Needless to say, sing songs of worship continuously until you sleep at night.

If you have abided the programme to this stage, then I say well done! You have completed the most difficult stage. You have, for three full days, avoided asking anything from God, but instead given to Him the only thing He desires, adoration.

Asking for things comes naturally but giving takes discipline and you have proved yourself disciplined and thus you qualify for the next stage.

Psalm 96

1 O sing unto the LORD a new song: sing unto the LORD, all the earth. 2 Sing unto the LORD, bless his name; shew forth his salvation from day to day. 3 Declare his glory among the heathen, his wonders among all people. 4 For the LORD is great, and greatly to be praised: he is to be feared above all gods. 5 For all the gods of the nations are idols: but the LORD made the heavens. 6 Honour and majesty are before him: strength and beauty are in his sanctuary. 7 Give unto the LORD, O ye kindreds of the people, give unto the LORD glory and strength. 8 Give unto the LORD the glory due unto his name: bring an offering, and come into his courts. 9 O worship the LORD in the beauty of holiness: fear before him, all the earth .10 Say among the heathen that the LORD reigneth: the world also shall be established that it shall not be moved: he shall judge the people righteously. 11 Let the heavens rejoice, and let the earth be glad; let the sea roar, and the fulness thereof. 12 Let the field be joyful, and all that is therein: then shall all the trees of the wood rejoice. 13 Before the LORD: for he cometh, for he cometh to judge the earth: he shall judge the world with righteousness, and the people with his truth.

Day 4

This is the first day for asking anything of God. The only thing you are allowed to ask of God on this day, is forgiveness. Spend the day asking God to forgive you for all the known sins you can recall. Ask for His forgiveness for the times you have failed Him in ministering to the needs of others and the Church. Ask for His forgiveness for your times of murmuring and failure to give praise.

Promise Him that you will change your ways and make amends wherever possible. Ask Him for grace to keep your mouth under control, your thoughts pure and your actions and motives sincere. Study the bible and sing songs of dedication and submission.

Psalm 51

1 Have mercy upon me, O God, according to thy lovingkindness: according unto the multitude of thy tender mercies blot out my transgressions. 2 Wash me thoroughly from mine iniquity, and cleanse me from my sin. 3 For I acknowledge my transgressions: and my sin is ever before me. 4 Against thee, thee only, have I sinned, and done this evil in thy sight: that thou mightest be justified when thou speakest, and be clear when thou judgest. 5 Behold, I was shapen in iniquity; and in sin did my mother conceive me. 6 Behold, thou desirest truth in the inward parts: and in the hidden part thou shalt make me to know wisdom.7 Purge me with hyssop, and I shall be clean: wash me, and I shall be whiter than snow. 8 Make me to hear joy and gladness; that the bones which thou hast broken may rejoice. 9 Hide thy face from my sins, and blot out all mine iniquities. 10 Create in me a clean heart, O God; and renew a right spirit within me. 11 Cast me not away from thy presence; and take not thy holy spirit from me. 12 Restore unto me the joy of thy salvation; and uphold me with thy free spirit. 13 Then will I teach transgressors thy ways; and sinners shall be converted unto thee. 14 Deliver me from bloodguiltiness, O God, thou God of my salvation: and my tongue shall sing aloud of thy righteousness. 15 O LORD, open thou my lips; and my mouth shall shew forth thy praise. 16 For thou desirest not sacrifice; else would I give it: thou delightest not in burnt offering. 17 The sacrifices of God are a broken spirit: a broken and a contrite heart, O God, thou wilt not despise. 18 Do good in thy good pleasure unto Zion: build thou the walls of Jerusalem. 19 Then shalt thou be pleased with the sacrifices of righteousness, with burnt offering and whole burnt offering: then shall they offer bullocks upon thine altar.

Day 5

<u>Job 23, verses 1-7</u>

1 Then Job answered and said, 2 Even to day is my complaint bitter: my stroke is heavier than my groaning. 3 Oh that I knew where I might find him! that I might come even to his seat! 4 I would order my cause before him, and fill my mouth with arguments. 5 I would know the words which he would answer me, and understand what he would say unto me. 6 Will he plead against me with his great power? No; but he would put strength in me. 7 There the righteous might dispute with him; so should I be delivered for ever from my judge.

Isaiah 1, verses 18-19

18 *Come now, and let us reason together, saith the LORD: though your sins be as scarlet, they shall be as white as snow; though they be red like crimson, they shall be as wool.* **19** *If ye be willing and obedient, ye shall eat the good of the land:*

Today, you get to be a lawyer. You now have the opportunity to engage your father intimately in discussion and respectfully insist on His performance of certain needs in your life. I want you to seclude yourself and get a pen and paper ready. Sit down and keep your eyes open if you like, kneel down or take any posture that suits you, believe that the Godhead is present with you.

There is no need to be afraid, even if it seems you are complaining or you sound bitter. You are merely pleading your cause before God. I want you to recount your disappointments to God. Explain to Him how embarrassed, disgraced, confused, disillusioned, and helpless you feel as a result of specific things you asked of Him but never received.

You may feel like crying or even feel that He let you down. Don't worry God knows how you feel anyway, so let yourself go, pour your heart out because you are in safe company and no harm will befall you.

Convince Him of why you believe those things should have been done for you. Show Him examples in the Bible where He did the same for others. For example, if you are barren, remind Him of Hannah, and make a vow of your own choice to Him if only He would grant your request. Use the example of Jabez if your situation seems completely hopeless. Now, I want you to record your conversations with Him throughout this day. Make sure your paper is dated, list your requests and number them. If they are time governed, explain to God that you are not dictating to Him, but merely giving an indication of the relevance of time to your request.

This is also an opportunity to ask God respectfully why He did not grant certain requests you made in the past. The chances are that you probably already know why, if you have adhered to the programme so far, but ask anyway; if only to verify that God is neither dead nor dumb.

Finally, present your list before Him like Hezekiah. I assure you that He can read. Always refer to that list until your requests are met and you have ticked off each item.

This is not a licence for greed; make sure you are asking God for things that are important to you and are within the scope of His will concerning you. Do not pray out of lust or covetousness as God is not mocked.

Day 6

Romans 8 verses 26-28

26 Likewise the Spirit also helpeth our infirmities: for we know not what we should pray for as we ought: but the Spirit itself maketh intercession for us with groanings which cannot be uttered. 27 And he that searcheth the hearts knoweth what is the mind of the Spirit, because he maketh intercession for the saints according to the will of God. 28 And we know that all things work together for good to them that love God, to them who are the called according to his purpose.

Today you should resume your normal prayer life. On day 5 you merely restated the things you had previously asked of God today; you can ask for new things that pertain to your daily living. Pray as led by the Holy Spirit and bask in the splendour or His grace and anointing.

Day 7

Psalm 40 verse 16

Let all those that seek thee rejoice and be glad in thee: let such as love thy salvation say continually, The LORD be magnified.

Celebrate your victory. If you like you may break at noon. Rejoice in Him and thank Him ceaselessly for giving you the strength to complete the programme and for answering your prayers.

Why the programme?

The programme is not a ritual, nor is it an exclusive formula for success. Any attempt to turn it into a religious rite will only result in failure, as God cannot be placed in a box. He does as He pleases and is not bound by my rules, or anybody's for that matter.

The programme is merely an attempt to teach you how to pray in a structured manner so that you may have results every time you pray. Many Christians simply rush in and out of God's presence, merely to ask for favours and never taking time to appreciate Him. If this prayer plan is not applicable to you, you do not have to follow it and I can assure you that God will continue to answer your prayer as long as you approach him in the proper manner.

Some people, however, need help and guidance in this area. Besides, there is nothing wrong with spiritual exercise.

Chapter 7

Will God Speak to Me?

One thing I want you to remember, is that nobody can dictate to God how to do things. If He decides to, He can hide things from us. No man has complete access to all of God's information. Even when your request relates to rigid issues, my advise is that you approach God with an open mind. Never insist to the point where you are so blinded that when God is speaking, you are not hearing Him or to the point when granting your request may become harmful to you; as demonstrated above when the Jews asked for food.

In 1 Kings 19 11 – 12, we see a demonstration of God's sovereignty in the ministry of Elijah:

11 And he said, Go forth, and stand upon the mount before the LORD. And, behold, the LORD passed by, and a great and strong wind rent the mountains, and brake in pieces the rocks before the LORD; but the LORD was not in the wind: and after the wind an earthquake; but the LORD was not in the earthquake: 12 And after the earthquake a fire; but the LORD was not in the fire: and after the fire a still small voice.

God reveals Himself to us in different ways. He chooses the best medium of communication for each child and for each occasion. Elijah was one of the mightiest prophets of the Old Testament and we know of his many exploits. Elijah commanded fire from heaven, declared a draught in the land, and took on the mighty Ahab and Jezebel alliance. The Bible foretold that the coming of John the Baptist would be in the spirit and power of Elijah. John's confrontational and bold approach in preaching the gospel confirmed this many generations later. At the time, when God spoke to Elijah in the portion of the scriptures above, Elijah was in great distress and needed to hear from God.

When God eventually answered Elijah, He elected the still small voice above the wind, the earthquake and the fire. This was no doubt strange territory for Elijah who was the fiery preacher and destroyer of all things evil. The still small voice was probably too timid an approach for Elijah to relate with.

Sometimes God communicates with us in ways we do not expect or are not used to. That is why we sometimes, when God is pointing in a particular direction, tend to miss the way. We simply are not objective enough or submissive enough to His will to do something different to what we are normally used to. Sometimes God will use certain people, preachers or even unbelievers to minister to our needs if we open up our minds to Him. God will not be dictated to, nor will He be intimidated by our narrow-mindedness. 1 Corinthians 12: 5-7 says:

And there are differences of administrations, but the same LORD. And there are diversities of operations, but it is the same

God which worketh all in all. But the manifestation of the Spirit is given to every man to profit withal.

God cannot be boxed-up and predicted. You cannot make any accurate forecasts about God. The Bible says that as the heaven is far above the earth so are His ways higher than ours.

Saul was kingly material, both in physical appearance and carriage. This led Samuel to conclude that the next anointed king would be of similar character. He was gravely wrong, as God elected a mere shepherd boy to be king instead. So you see even great men of God can get it wrong.

The best way to approach God is in a non-prescriptive manner. Go to Him with a blank piece of paper and not your pre-planned agenda which may not necessarily fit into His plans. Don't say to God, 'give me X, Y or Z', rather tell Him you'd like X, Y or Z but only if He approves. Then when God responds, you would be more receptive to Him as His options will always be better than your choices. Then it would not make any difference to you whether God speaks through the wind, the earthquake or the fire because you have asked for His will to be done.

My closing words are these. Strictly speaking, God is the only one who decides what requests will be granted or otherwise. Do not allow people to sell religion to you by saying that your request is not God's will for you; you have a right to ask your father directly, through the prayer plan above, or through your own tried and tested method. I repeat, I am not prescribing a formulae for success, I merely offer you a structured method for finding out why it seems your requests have been ignored by God.

God always speaks to His children and He can do any of the following if you take time out to speak Him:

1. Simply grant your request with or without explanation.

2. Give you an explanation as to why you did not get your answer and may not or may still get it.

3. Say no.

4. Say yes, but wait.

5. Say yes and give priority to your request because of your perseverance.

6. Say no and provide a suitable or better alternative; never an inferior alternative.

7. Any possible set of combinations from options above.

May the Lord keep you and bless you. May He grant you the stamina and courage to wait on Him with passion and desperate perseverance until your prayers are answered. Amen.